THE TOUCH OF A MOTH

THE TOUCH OF A MOTH

THE 35TH ANNUAL HAIKU CANADA MEMBERS' ANTHOLOGY

Edited by
Claudia Coutu Radmore and Marco Fraticelli

ScrivenerPress

Library and Archives Canada Cataloguing in Publication

The Touch of a Moth / editors: Claudia Coutu Radmore and Marco Fraticelli.

(Annual Haiku Canada members' anthology ; 35)
ISBN 978-1-896350-50-9

1. Haiku, Canadian (English). 2. Canadian poetry (English)--21st century. 3. Haiku, English. I. Radmore, Claudia Coutu, 1943- II. Fraticelli, Marco, 1945- III. Haiku Canada IV. Series: Haiku Canada members' anthology ; 35

PS8285.H3T68 2012   C811'.0410806   C2012-901090-1

Book design: Laurence Steven
Cover design: Chris Evans
Cover illustration: Heather A. MacDonald
Interior illustrations: Dorothy Howard

Published by Scrivener Press
465 Loach's Road,
Sudbury, Ontario, Canada, P3E 2R2
info@yourscrivenerpress.com   www.scrivenerpress.com

We acknowledge the financial support of the Ontario Arts Council, the Canada Council for the Arts, and the Government of Canada through the Canada Book Fund for our publishing activities.

ONTARIO ARTS COUNCIL
CONSEIL DES ARTS DE L'ONTARIO

Canada Council
for the Arts

Conseil des Arts
du Canada

Canadian
Heritage

Patrimoine
canadien

Dedicated to all Haiku Canada members
who have passed away

Preface

There was a time in the early days of Haiku Canada when we were ecstatic about the possibility of having 25 paying members. Now, as we approach our 35th year, our membership is over several hundred. It is hoped that this anthology reflects the state of Haiku Canada today. Within these pages are haiku by current members as well as poems by members who have passed away. Some haiku reflect many years spent in a haiku-writing life. Other poems are written by members who have only recently discovered haiku.

We've included a few photos and anecdotes to fill in the Haiku Canada story and would have loved to have had space for more. The undated photos are from the 1980s.

Many thanks to our archivist, Dorothy Howard, for her time and input, and especially for her ink designs that so perfectly punctuate these pages.

The artwork of Heather MacDonald has graced our anthology covers for several years. This year we asked her for a 'mark', rather than a complete image. We wanted to identify with the Japanese roots of haiku, tanka and various related forms, but haiku by Canadian poets has now become recognizably Canadian and not so Japanese in character. Her response is, we believe, perfect.

Since Haiku Canada has become more bilingual over the years in our publications, in the Haiku Canada Review, the e-Newsletter, and with the launch of the Villeneuve Award, we hope that this anthology reflects the bilingual nature of Canada.

As with any project of this type, the help of many people was necessary for its successful completion. We would especially like to thank Terry Ann Carter for her help, and George Swede for allowing Terry to extract the Haiku Canada history from an essay of hers published in *frogpond*. We would also like to take this opportunity to thank Agnes Jackle who has, for so many years, been handling our finances.

Finally, we owe much to Carol Stephen, Philomene Kocher, and Carolanne Reynolds for checking the manuscript and helping to get it ready for publication, and especially to Janice Bowie of Lux Photo in Carleton Place who worked with the archived photos so we could use them.

Marco Fraticelli and Claudia Coutu Radmore
Editors

A Brief History of Haiku Canada

Publications of Canadian pioneer haiku poets Claire Pratt and Rod Willmot, Eric Amann's critical essay *The Wordless Poem*, published haiku of the celebrated Beat poets, and Cor van den Heuvel's *The Haiku Anthology* (1974) which was the first collection of English-language haiku by a major publisher (Anchor Books/Doubleday) were influences which soon led to the formation of the Haiku Society of Canada. The group was founded on the night of October 21, 1977, at Nikko Gardens, a now defunct Japanese restaurant in Toronto's Chinatown. Four persons were present: Eric Amann, a friend of his, George Swede, and Betty Drevniok. Eric Amann was given the duties of the first president and newsletter editor, and Betty volunteered to be the treasurer. In fall, 1977, Eric Amann encouraged George Swede to edit a strictly Canadian anthology of haiku. After approaching Three Trees in Toronto, a press already interested in his own work, the *Canadian Haiku Anthology* was born (1979), featuring twenty poets from coast to coast with work ranging in style from 5-7-5 to visual haiku. The anthology received significant recognition for haiku. It was launched in May 1980 in Toronto's prestigious Harbourfront, Canada's premier literary festival and reading venue. After a day-long haiku festival with related art displays and calligraphy demonstrations, ten poets read to a sold-out audience.

At the 1981 annual general meeting at Betty Drevniok's home in Combermere, Ontario, on Thanksgiving weekend, the idea for another anthology was born. After a reading of exceptionally fine erotic haiku by Cor van den Heuvel (up from Manhattan), George Swede, Rod Willmot, André Duhaime, Marshall Hryciuk, and Margaret Saunders, George suggested to Rod that he edit a collection of erotic haiku. In two years, Black Moss Press in Windsor, Ontario published this collection. Although two-thirds of the contributors were from the United States, the idea, the editor and the publisher were Canadian. It was also launched at Harbourfront in May 1983. This anthology continues to be one of a kind in English-language haiku.

In 1985, a third landmark collection appeared. It was the brain-child of Quebec poets Dorothy Howard and André Duhaime: *Haïku: anthologie canadienne/Canadian Anthology*. An ambitious book, it included 65 poets from both English- and French-speaking Canada, as well as poets from the Japanese community. Every haiku was rendered in French and English, and in the case of the Japanese contributors, in Japanese as well. As if these innovations weren't enough, the anthology also contained illuminating histories of the English-language haiku in North America by Elizabeth Searle Lamb, and the French-language haiku in Quebec and France by Bernadette Guilmette.

By this time, the Haiku Canada weekends had moved to the monastery in Aylmer, Quebec, with provisions directed by Dorothy Howard and later Ruby Spriggs. Prominent poets from the monastery years also included Grant Savage, Hans Jongman, Marshall Hryciuk, and Marianne Bluger. Marianne was instrumental in bringing a constitution to Haiku Canada and laboured for many years on the project; she worked closely with Muriel Ford (Toronto) on the writing and advocacy of this important documentation. Marianne also brought an aesthetic to the meetings in Aylmer and later, Carleton University. A first-class gardener, she always arrived with boughs—

sometimes entire branches of blossoms in her arms—tulips, daffodils, and other spring flowers for the Haiku Canada Weekends which were traditionally held on the long weekends in May. With Betty Drevniok, Margaret Saunders, Muriel Ford, Dorothy Howard, anne mckay, Anita Krumins, and Sandra Fuhringer, Marianne was an important female voice in the development of English-language haiku in Canada, and by the 90s was a strong influence on newer female poets. Karen Sohne added her brilliant voice to the Canadian chorus when she made a permanent move north.

Other French-Canadian haiku voices included Jocelyne Ville-neuve (1941-1998) who will be honoured by Haiku Canada with the Jocelyne Villeneuve Award for French-speaking haiku poets (the first winners will be known in 2012); André Duhaime, Micheline Be-audry; and Janick Belleau who publishes in French with translations into English.

Haiku Canada is a well-run organization with a constitution, a list of officers, and a publishing branch that first produced the *Haiku Canada Newsletter* edited by LeRoy Gorman. An online version of the newsletter is offered with Marco Fraticelli at the helm. The *Haiku Canada Review*, still with its legendary editor LeRoy Gorman, is produced twice a year (a winter/spring issue and a summer/fall issue). Since 2007, the *Haiku Canada Review* dedicates some of its pages to French haiku; this section is coordinated by Micheline Beaudry. The *Haiku Canada Members' Anthology*, introduced at each Haiku Canada Weekend, is now edited by Claudia Coutu Radmore.

Perhaps the most influential figure in the formative years of the haiku movement in Canada was Toronto medical doctor/poet Eric Amann. He founded the magazine *Haiku* and was its editor for three years. Under Amann's editorship *Haiku* rapidly became one of the most influential North American periodicals, publishing experimental as well as classical work. After a hiatus of seven years, during which he engaged in other kinds of writing, Amann returned to haiku with a new magazine *Cicada* which immediately achieved a similar status. In 1982, Amann curtailed his haiku activities once again. During this year, Toronto poets Keith Southward and Marshall Hryciuk inaugurated *Inkstone* which appeared over the next ten years. The periodical became known for its hard-hitting but well-reasoned reviews. Although *Inkstone* ceased publication in the early 90s, Dorothy Howard's *RAW NerVZ HAIKU* continued to provide a place for Canadian and international poets to publish their edgier poems. The graphic influences of both Dorothy and Ruby Spriggs enhanced early publications and newsletters. Ruby was well-known for her line drawings and small doodles; she also created large canvases with acrylics to enhance her haiku. Both Marianne Bluger and Ruby Spriggs died of breast cancer within two years of each other. It was a great sorrow for those in the Haiku Canada community.

George Swede is another significant pioneer in the early days of haiku development in Canada. Born in Riga, Latvia, George came to Canada with his mother and stepfather after the Second World War. After earning degrees in psychology from UBC and Dalhousie, George settled in Toronto for an academic career at Ryerson Polytechnic Institute, now Ryerson University. It is the numbers around George's contribution to the development of haiku in Canada (and the world) that always astonish. He has published over 2,000 poems in over 7,000 places. His poems have been translated into 21 languages; he edited three anthologies: *The Canadian Haiku Anthology* (Three Trees Press, 1979); *Cicada Voices, the Selected Haiku of Eric Amann* (High/Coo Press, 1983); and with co-editor Randy Brooks, *Global Haiku 25 Poets Worldwide* (Iron Press, 2000). George was consulting editor for eight anthologies. He has written 94 articles on poetry and 17 on psychology; he has written 13 children's books and two psychology texts. He has had five gallery shows for his haiga and is the current Editor (with Anita Krumins, Assistant Editor) of *frogpond: The Journal of the Haiku Society of America.*

Betty Drevniok, also a major contributor to the early development of haiku in Canada, was born in the United States, and relocated to Toronto as a nurse shortly after World War II. She discovered haiku in the late 60s through her work with sumi-e brush painting. In 1976, under her haiku name Makato, she published *Inland—Three Rivers from an Ocean.* In 1980 she organized the first International Haiku Society of Canada meeting in Toronto. Several Festivals of the Falling Leaves followed in Combermere where she lived. Betty was the secretary of the society for the first two years, and president for the next three. In 1993 she published a final individual collection *Thoughts of Spring* (Hexagram Series, King's Road Press, Montreal). Since 2002 (five years after her death), Haiku Canada honours her memory through the Betty Drevniok Annual Haiku Award.

Marco Fraticelli, an early luminary, travelled from Montreal to join the like-minded poets at Combermere. Writing haiku for over thirty years, Marco has published poems in many anthologies and publications. In 1988, he inherited money from his grandmother and (in Marco's words):

> instead of blowing the money or paying off some bills, I started the Hexagram Series and King's Road Press. I was distressed by the terrible haiku that was appearing in print. I decided to seek out poets whose work I admired and asked them to send me their entire body of work. From these, I selected 20 or so best ones. The point was to provide a series of inexpensive ($2.00) books that one could offer to anyone new to haiku as a model to work from. The first one in 1991 was by

LeRoy Gorman, "glass bell," followed by Alexis Rotella. Other poets include: George Swede, Nick Avis, Ruby Spriggs, Dorothy Howard, Karen Sohne, Jean Jorgensen, Marshall Hryciuk, Dee Evetts, Michael Dylan Welch and others.

Marco was instrumental in the holographic (written by hand, as in holographic will) anthologies to commemorate anniversaries for Haiku Canada. The first *Holographic Anthology* appeared in 1987 for the 10th anniversary, then 1992, 1997, 2004 (with Philomene Kocher), and 2007 (with Philomene Kocher). In 2012 for the 35th anniversary, he will edit the sixth Holographic Anthology with Marshall Hryciuk. In 2006, he founded the *Haiku Canada Electronic Newsletter* and continues to be its editor. In 2008 he was English co-editor (with Terry Ann Carter) and Francine Chicoine (French editor) of *Carpe Diem: Anthologie canadienne du haïku / Canadian Anthology of Haiku*, a collaborative publication of Borealis Press and Les Éditions David.

Dorothy Howard, illustrator, calligrapher, editor, translator, educator, book maker, former co-president (1985-1988) and president (1988-1990) of Haiku Canada, was an active contributor to early Haiku Canada events and publications. She organized Haiku Canada Weekends at the monastery in Aylmer, co-edited with André Duhaime, *Haïku: anthologie canadienne/Canadian Anthology* (Éditions Asticou). From 1994-2007 she edited *RAW NerVZ HAIKU*, and *casse-pieds* since 2006. In November 2006, she published Amann's *The Wordless Poem* translated into French by Daniel Py. Dorothy is the memory of Haiku Canada as she remains its archivist to this day. Volumes of books, pamphlets, newsletters, broadsheets, and art works line the walls of her home in Aylmer, Quebec. Her collection *the photographer's shadow* was published in the Hexagram Series (King's Road Press, 1999).

Making his mark as an outstanding editor of national as well as international fame, LeRoy Gorman contributed to the growth and interest of haiku in Canada with his own haiku moving into the aesthetics of the experimental, the concrete, the visual poem. His minimalist poems have been appearing in print for over thirty years. LeRoy has published poetry with Guernica Press, Éditions Asticou, Nietzsche's Brolly, Proof Press, King's Road Press, and Timberline. Over the years he has assumed or written under at least 50 pseudonyms. Since 1996 he has been editor of the Haiku Canada publications: *Haiku Canada Newsletter* 1996-2006, the *Haiku Canada Review* beginning in 2007, as well as annual broadsheets for Haiku Canada members. In 1998 he began to publish poetry leaflets and postcards under his *pawEpress* imprint.

For twenty years, Toronto poet and book marketer, Marshall Hryciuk, has been writing haiku and winning international awards. At the Haiku International Association symposium in Tokyo (2009) he presented his collection *Arizona to Crete* (Imago Press, 2008). The poems were translated into Japanese and posted on the HIA website. Other publications, among many, include *Singed Leaves: A Book of Haiku Poetry* (Dundurn Press, 1990) and *Persimmon Moons* (Imago Press, 1998). His partner Karen Sohne operates Red Iron Press which publishes haiku in small handmade, folded broadsheets. Together they organize the annual "Late Night Renku Parties" at all Haiku Canada weekends, with Marshall serving as renku master.

By the year 2000, major cities were hosting haiku groups across the country. Some of the poets belonging to these groups are Haiku Canada members; others are not. Pacifi-kana (British Columbia and Yukon), Magpie Poets (Alberta), Deer Park (Toronto), which no longer meets, KaDo Ottawa, French-speaking and English-speaking groups co-existing in Montreal, and HaikuQuébec (Quebec City).

In eastern Canada, it is a one-man show with Nick Avis in St. John's, Newfoundland, at the helm of the Haiku Canada boat. Nick was present at some of the early meetings in Combermere and the monastery, and served as President of Haiku Canada for six years. His poetry has been published nationally and internationally for thirty years. His chapbook *footprints* from the *Hexagram Series* (King's Road Press, 1993) won a Haiku Society of America award.

This past year, Nick singlehandedly organized the Haiku Canada Weekend at Memorial University in Saint John's which also included a trip on a fishing boat to Cape Spear. Imagine twenty haiku poets, three Newfoundland fishermen, and the boat's owner, out on the sea admiring puffins, northern and western sea eagles, gulls, hawks, ospreys, albatross plus many more. Later, there was a gathering at Nick's home for drinks, late night snacks and renku.

A Newfoundland "house party" he called it. Marco Fraticelli commented that it reminded him of "the early years" at Combermere.

This year, Haiku Canada is celebrating its 35th anniversary in Toronto—where it all began. Festivities will include a new haiku anthology (edited by Marco Fraticelli and Claudia Coutu Radmore), a new holographic anthology (edited by Marco and Marshall), a collection of Drevniok Award winners edited by Mike Montreuil, readings, papers, ginkgo walks, presentations, workshops, and late-night parties orchestrated by Marshall and Karen. Even though it will not be a Festival of Falling Leaves, it will be a warm and congenial gathering. Join Haiku Canada for the biggest party yet!

Terry Ann Carter
Ottawa
2011

With thanks to George Swede who has let Terry Ann extract this Haiku Canada history from an article she wrote for *frogpond*, "Internment Camp to Contemporary Landscapes: A History of Haiku in Canada".

THE TOUCH OF A MOTH

November rain—
the dreary hum of traffic
dampens

past the chimney
December stars
shiver

Stephen Addiss, a scholar-artist-poet, is Tucker-Boatwright Professor
at the University of Richmond. His own haiku as well as translations
have appeared in many magazines, journals, and books. His calligraphy
and paintings, including haiga, have been exhibited in Asia, Europe,
and the United States.

Snow falling
   on the empty parking lot:
     Christmas eve...

In the quiet pond
even the touch of a moth
shatters the full moon

Cicada Voices
HIGH/COO PRESS 1983

Eric Amann was one of the founders of Haiku Canada and the author of *The Wordless Poem*.

coucher du soleil
un castor traverse le lac
en ligne droite

soleil de carte postale
une brise
m'appelle au lac

Bernard Anton vit dans les Laurentides. Il a publié plusieurs livres
(poésie, conte, slam, essai). Son thème de prédilection est la nature. Il
est un amoureux inconditionnel de la beauté de la nature. Son recueil
de haiku *Laurentïdes* est publié aux éditions Humanitas en 2004.

For quite a while, Jacob Harris was Haiku Canada's youngest member. His mother, Angela Leuck, has been vice-president of Haiku Canada for several years.

12th century Portuguese castle—
computer
prints ticket

Hummingbird, September 2002

not opening
indoors
the last rose of summer

Asahi Haikuist Network, 2002

I have been writing haiku and short poems for nearly 30 years. I have always lived in Toronto and my poems are inspired both by city life and holiday travel, often to Algonquin Park, Maine and Portugal.

evening shadows
beach stones tumble
into drift

frost
thistle blue
tidewater

Cheryl Ashley lives on a small island in the Salish Sea.

gouttes de pluie
abritée sous le porche
écouter le temps

saut sur les roches
pour traverser le torrent
cœur d'enfant

Ma passion: l'écriture. Mes textes ont été lus lors de cabarets littéraires et publiés dans la revue de la Fédération Québécoise du Loisir Littéraire. Une nouvelle fait partie du recueil de la Fédération des Aînés du Québec. 3ᵉ prix du concours de haïku du Sénégal 2010.

lost
in my binoculars
a bird calls

Modern Haiku, summer 2010

sparrows
in a clear sky
ice in the birdbath

Munira Judith Avinger has published four books with Borealis Press: *The Empty Bowl / Le Bol Vide*, *Lifting The Veil / Soulever Le Voile*, *Julia* and *Hidden/Caché*. She has also published haiku and tanka in several journals, including *Haiku Canada*, *Gusts* and *Modern Haiku*.

back from her walk
    she brings the autumn chill
        to bed

frogpond, 33.1, p.27.

into a north east wind
    the last remaining headstone
leans toward the sea

Poetic Justice, Law Foundation of NL,
St. John's, NL, 2006.

Nick Avis's haiku, poetry and criticism have been published for over 30 years. He is a former president of Haiku Canada; and his chapbook, *footprints,* won an HSA Merit Book Award.

Halloween
the pumpkin fills
with rain

deep white drifts—
this snow that fell
while I slept

Member of Haiku Canada since 2007. Trying to learn all I can about
this deceptively simple art and produce something passable. Currently
finding inspiration in the haiku of Santoka Taneda.

a man in black
with a black umbrella
walks down the alley

sitting in a chair
by the kitchen window
just watching clouds

Winona Baker wrote seven books; won haiku and tanka awards; is in over 90 anthologies in North America, Europe, New Zealand and Japan; had poems translated into Japanese, Croatian, French, Greek, Yugoslavian and Romanian. Her most recent book is *Nature Here is Half Japanese* (2010).

MIKE MONTREUIL

You could tell we weren't from the Rock.

It was a dark and gloomy day, damp and cold. And being the city slickers we were and are, many of us only had sweaters and light jackets. You'd think that would have been more than enough for a boat cruise to a seabird island.

The crew started handing out one piece survival suits. My first reaction was, what on earth for? But we all took it in stride and donned our suits. Not from the Rock, there we were, dressed in day-glo orange, looking like astronauts waiting to have their helmets strapped on.

Earth calling Marco! He wasn't listening. He was a kid again, both hands on the boat's external ship's wheel, smiling for the cameras. If only he had been allowed to steer.

We were all warm and dry in our suits and all we could do is laugh at each other. Yup, city slickers. I wonder what the puffins and gulls thought of these orange beings bobbing up and down. On our way back to shore, many of us wound up in the cabin. You can only take so much wind and spray. Our barkeeper said the swells were only a meter high. Hmmm… To me they looked more like two meters.

A tumbler of screech and ginger ale warmed our hearts. Salut! to a great cruise.

autumn light
just this much
to go on

The Betty Drevniok Award, 2009,
First Place

butterfly...
I rephrase
the question

Modern Haiku 42.2

Francine Banwarth, editor of *frogpond* and a co-founder of Haiku
Dubuque, leads haiku workshops at The Foundry Books in Wisconsin.
Second vice-president of the Haiku Society of America 2008-2011,
her haiku and senryu have been published widely. "I try to be present
in the moment and cultivate a haiku mind."

bird-feeder birds
feeding ground feeders
below

a lull in the rain
a goldfinch hops and sips
along the branch

Retired Engineer.

in the urban battle field...
the young man
confronts rent

on the first floor of a 48-storey office building...
an immigrant caretaker
daydreams

Shaunt Basmajian was a founder of the Canadian Poetry Association,
co-founder of Old Nun Publications, and was a member of the
Parliament Street Library poetry group. The Shaunt Basmajian
Chapbook Award, given annually to a Canadian poet, was established
in his memory. The contest ran from 1996-2008.

Shaunt Basmajian,
a founding member of
Haiku Canada

killing field
buttercups cling
to my shoe

Haiku Ireland Kukai *17*,
1st Prize

mother's day
she puts me
on hold

HSA Brady Senryu Contest 2010,
2nd Prize

Roberta Beary's book of short poems, *The Unworn Necklace* (Snapshot Press, 2011) was selected as a William Carlos Williams Book Award finalist by the Poetry Society of America. Her website is www.robertabeary.com

soleil de mars
un café bu dans la neige
le manteau ouvert

March sun
drinking coffee in the snow
coat wide open

Born in Montreal, Micheline Beaudry lives in Boucherville, Quebec, Canada. She has participated in many haiku anthologies like the 55th Bashô anthology. She published *Blanche Mémoire, Les couleurs du vent*, at Les Éditions David. She founded GHM—Groupe de haïku de Montréal in 2005.

jour de pluie
chantant sur le lac
couple de huards

rainy day
singing on the lake
loon mates

Janick Belleau: Poet, cultural writer & lecturer. Main publications:
A tanka collection (Canada-Japan 2010 Award), *D'âmes et d'ailes /
of souls and wings*; editor of *Regards de femmes—haïkus francophones*;
coeditor of *L'Érotique poème court/haïku*. Bilingual web site:
www.janickbelleau.ca

garden path
stone Buddha reflecting
bright sunlight

on this dark night
who else is watching stars
alone outside

Sheila Bello lives in Toronto. Her published works include a volume
of poetry. She joined Haiku Canada in 2001.

coffee shop lineup
watching an ant
circle a poppy seed

Cross Currents Handbook, Ottawa 2009
Haiku North America Conference

puppet show
I applaud
a block of wood

DailyHaiku Cycle, 7 April 2009

Patricia Benedict is Professor Emeritus from the University of
Calgary and has been writing and publishing haiku for many years.
She received Honourable Mention in the Betty Drevniok Award
1998. She lives in Calgary.

a single leaf
this shadow and that shadow
falling

January
Santa on the front lawn
deflated

Maxianne Berger lives in Montréal.

hearing the call
of the Mourning Dove—
I follow the trail

at the fountain
a Sparrow is drinking—
      I wait

I was born and raised in Toronto, Ontario. Early in my life, my lyrics
were published, but it was not until my senior years that I read and
wrote haiku and joined the haiku group in Toronto for further study.
I moved to Alexandria, Ontario, recently.

blowing bubbles...
how peacefully they float
above the ramparts

all the prayer slips
crammed in the Wailing Wall
where do they go?

An international prize-winning haiku poet, Rick Black wrote these poems after a visit to Israel with his wife and seven-year-old daughter. He recently moved to Arlington, Virginia, where he will continue to run Turtle Light Press.

dazed with cold
a bumblebee clings
to a faded aster

HCN X. 2 1997

behind the church
discarded lilies
in the morning sun

Tamarack & Clearcut,
Carleton University Press, 1997

After living in Montreal, Toronto and New York, Marianne Bluger
settled in Ottawa a half mile from where she was born. Her collected
haiku, *Tamarack and Clearcut,* was published by Carleton University
Press.

Emiko Miyashita

The Japan Foundation sponsored me to read at the 25th Anniversary Haiku Canada Weekend held in Toronto on May 18th, 2002. It meant a lot to me to be able to join the stream of Canadian haiku for I thought it was a cool thing to do! Right after that, LeRoy made my very first haiku collection, *to the Milky Way* (pawEprint 49, June 2002), and then Marco did my first haiku book, *a mime's perpendicular pause* (King's Road Press, 2005). I feel like I am growing up with you. A Happy Birthday, Haiku Canada!

Deep Bow,
Emiko

overtaking
the funeral procession
the garbage truck

walking
like an old man
my shadow

Peter Brady was born in New York City and raised in upstate New York. He immigrated to Canada in 1967 and settled in the province of Quebec. In 1986, he began writing haiku. He is currently working on a collection for publication.

dandelions
and crabgrass together—
almost summer

Sweven, Dec., 1978

a few scraps of wood
in his front yard—
day of the funeral

blackberries, 2011

Allan Brown had two haiku published in the journal *Mountain* in 1962.
Since then about 300 more have come out in Canadian and American
forums and are partly collected in his books *What Day Is It?* (2004), *a
penny in the grass* (2006) and *blackberries* (2011).

suddenly
at dusk five deer
winter thin

> *Tidepools: Haiku on Gabriola,*
> 2011

black night...
my kiss finds a dimple
on your shoulder

Bob Butkus has been writing haiku since 1995 when he boldly taught
its English form to his college students in Tokyo. He recently published
Godless Religion: Finding the Profound, which finds the haiku moment
within the profound.

falling leaves
now you know
I can change my mind

endless rain
in my mother's kitchen
the snap, snapping of beans

Terry Ann Carter is the author of *Lighting the Global Lantern: A Teacher's Guide to Writing Haiku and Related Literary Forms* available on amazon.com, and *Hallelujah* (Buschekbooks) haiku, senryu and tanka translated into French by Mike Montreuil. She has also published three collections of lyric poetry.

giving way
to constant pressure—
the riverbank

the perfect snowflake
ruined by the warmth
of my hand

A haiku neophyte, Darrell is attracted to haiku for its focus on emotion, nature and the seasons. He also loves the power that a haiku, when properly written, creates through its brevity.

Tom Clausen

One of my favorite HC memories involved a meeting with Marianne Bluger along the canal in Ottawa to go over tanka we were judging for a contest.

I had never met Marianne before and was quite excited at the chance to actually meet. I had admired her poetry for many years and exchanged some letters in which we shared the rather amazing background of our mothers having been best friends while at college at McGill in Montreal. I had heard my mother often mention Ruth Bluger and would see cards and letters that she sent bearing interesting Canadian stamps.

When I first became interested in haiku and then tanka I discovered that there was a Canadian poet named Marianne Bluger. Sure enough it was Ruth's daughter. I had no idea what Marianne might share about her mom and my mom but a meeting was something I had felt for a long time was meant to be.

We sat on a bench along the canal. It was a timelessly special spell of sharing family stories and tanka talk as if we were long friends already familiar with something very common and beautifully shared.

Bath

cutting a bruise
from the last peach—
your broken promise

Presence, #37, 2009

autumn equinox
we each make one
side of the bed

White Lotus, #7, 2008

Susan Constable finds most of her inspiration along the forest trails
and beaches of Vancouver Island, BC. Since 2006, her haiku, tanka,
haiga and haibun have been published in over 30 journals and in
numerous anthologies, including *New Resonance 6* and *Montage: The
Book.*

steep climb
I envy
the butterfly

red tulip—
a ladybug escapes
the blazing heat

Ellen Cooper, a mathematics teacher in Montreal, joined Haiku
Canada in 2000. After many publications, she received an honourable
mention in the Betty Drevniok Award of 2011. Haiku has provided an
outlet through which she could share her appreciation for nature and
passion for the outdoors.

snowmelt—
a running brook
reflects the clouds

broken spider web—
a ray of sunlight
hangs from the ceiling

Pamela Cooper has been writing haiku since 2000. Her haiku have appeared in several anthologies; among them, *Fuchsia Snowflakes* (2001), *Sun Through the Blinds* (2003), and *Tulip Haiku* (2004). Honourable mentions (Betty Drevniok Award, Mainichi Contest); finalist (VCBF Haiku Invitational 2011). Co-editor of *Montreal—A Haiku Anthology* (2010).

one of the editors

on the yellow center
of a lilac flower
centering myself

Poet in the Garden:
Angela Leuck.blogspot.com

darkness
the only thing big enough
to hide an ocean

Global Lantern, 2011

Claudia Coutu Radmore has been writing Japanese-form poetry since the mid nineties. Author of several books of lyric and Japanese-form poetry, on the editorial boards of *The Bywords Quarterly Journal* and *Arc* magazine, Claudia helps select tanka for *Gusts.* www.claudiacouturadmore.ca

Larry Neily and Marianne Bluger

still green
just when I thought I knew
autumn

bits of itself,
HSA Membership Anthology, 2002

bonfire's glow
my niece cups her hands
around a firefly

tempslibres, ed Serge Tome, 2003

Dina E. Cox is a poet, musician, and occasional freelancer whose poetry has been published in various anthologies and periodicals including *Simply Haiku, haigaonline, RAW NerVZ HAIKU, Modern English Tanka, LYNX* and *Carpe Diem* (Les Éditions David and Borealis Press). She won the Betty Drevniok Award in 2000.

April playground
only the teacher
wears a coat

heat wave—
the cow's udder
hangs in the pond

I have been a member of Haiku Canada since 2000 and have served as president since 2005. I enjoy the colour that haiku sensitivity brings to everyday events. Birds, cows, insects, flowers—all have inspired many haiku moments if not an actual haiku.

JANICK BELLEAU

Montréal, 2010. It was a great moment for Haiku Canada since it was our first completely bilingual Haiku Canada Weekend conference. We had unique surroundings at McGill University, illuminating lectures or workshops in English by Dorothy Howard, Rod Willmot, George Swede, Angela Leuck, and Terry Ann Carter, *communications mémorables d'André Duhaime, Jeanne Painchaud, Micheline Beaudry, Luce Pelletier, l'artiste Claire Dufresne ainsi que des membres de HaikuQuébec et du Groupe Haïku Montréal. En tant que présentatrice, j'étais véritablement excitée par cet événement et fière de l'apport de la Francophonie.*

Sneaking a peek
At the old corner window
Morning light

Snow sprinkled
A half eaten crabapple
Left on the doormat

Insatiablement curieuse, je suis enchantée par ce qui m'entoure quotidiennement surtout sachant que seul l'éphémère dure. Ma première passion est la photographie, jeu d'ombres de lumières. Écrire est une respiration et ce tout en ayant les yeux ouverts et fermés en même temps!

deadheading irises...
dew washes
my purple fingers

Mayfly

waiting room silence...
the surgeon's approach
on green paper feet

frogpond

I was born in Schenectady, New York. My husband and I have lived
in Alabama, North Carolina, Arkansas, Virginia, Massachusetts, New
Hampshire, Oregon, and Australia. We are now happily settled in
Maine with our three wonderful dogs.

rain washed wall
    the shadow of a pitchfork
        and the afternoon sun

a bee is droning
somewhere in the sleeves
of a scarecrow

Tom Dawe has been a high school teacher, English professor, visual
artist, editor, writer and poet. He has published seventeen volumes,
including poetry, folklore and children's literature. Elected to the
Newfoundland and Labrador Arts Council Hall of Honour, he was
also named St. John's Poet Laureate.

first snow
the broken beach chair
frozen to the ground

empty fair grounds
just me
and the cricket

Raffael de Gruttola is a founding member of the Boston Haiku Society
in 1988 and a past President of HSA. Editor of the *Boston Haiku News*
from 1988 to 2011, he has been invited on three occasions to Japan to
read and write haiku and renku.

retirement home—
each time the heron comes
another goldfish gone

Betty Drevniok Award, 2009
Honourable Mention

night rain
outside my window
the soft thud of a papaya

Haiku Society of America
Members' Anthology, 2004

Elehna de Sousa was born and raised in Hong Kong and came to
Canada in 1967 to further her studies. She currently lives on Salt
Spring Island, B.C. where she finds an abundance of inspiration for
her creative interests in poetry, mixed-media art, and photography.

prendre un grand *respir*
au milieu du champ de trèfles
pour s'en souvenir

conduite de nuit –
coup d'œil au rétroviseur
suivi par la lune

Mention honorable
au 12ᵉ Concours de haïkus du Mainichi,
Osaka, Japon, 2008

Née à Asbestos en 1956 avec une espérance de vie jusqu'en 2056;
poète, haïjin, auteur d'une dizaine d'ouvrages, elle a reçu une centaine
de prix littéraires au Québec, en France, en Roumanie, au Liban et
au Japon et publiée dans maintes anthologies. www.dianedescoteaux.
com

Marco Fraticelli

By the time I pulled up in front of Betty Drevniok's home, I was in a state of total panic.

It was sometime in the 70s and I had just driven seven hours from Montreal to attend my first Haiku Canada conference. In those days, the conferences were held at Betty's cabins in Combermere. With each hour that passed on the trip, I became more nervous. At the time, I was very new to the world of haiku and had decided to attend the conference in the hope of learning more about it.

For several years, I had been writing short poems which bore a passing resemblance to the haiku that I had seen in magazines like *frogpond*, but I still couldn't get a grasp on what a haiku was supposed to be. This conference was going to change all that. Finally I was going to learn the secrets of the haiku. I knew that the meeting was going to be attended by many notable haiku poets. These were poets whose names I had seen in all the major haiku magazines.

Somehow, I had expected a large gathering; one in which I could disappear into the crowd. Instead, what I found was a small group of maybe a dozen people who were standing, with wine glasses in hand, at Betty's living room window and staring back at me. I never even turned off the engine. After what seemed like a very long time of us staring at each other, I turned the car around and drove away. Fortunately, after I'd driven about twenty kilometres towards home, I managed to get a grip on myself and decided to drive back to Betty's. Years later, I found out that those who were there that day had quite a chuckle at my expense. However, when I did arrive back at Betty's and forced myself to enter her home, I was greeted by the warmth and hospitality which continues to this day at all the Haiku Canada conferences.

In thirty or so years since that first meeting, I have attended almost all of the Haiku Canada conferences. Although many of them have, for various reasons, been memorable, I doubt that any one image sticks in my mind more than the one of me looking through my windshield at those poets who were staring back at me through Betty's window.

(1919-1997)

my footprints on sand
another wave
   another wave

harvest moon
the child I was
in an antique frame

With Eric Amann and George Swede, a founder of Haiku Canada, and the host of the first few Haiku Canada Weekends in Combermere, Ontario. In 1980, Betty directed some of the haiku events at Toronto's Harbourfront Centre prior to readings from the *Canadian Haiku Anthology*.

Indian summer
berries on the dogwood
we thought had died

marching band
morning sun fills
the tuba's bell

Cathy Drinkwater Better is an award-winning poet and journalist
and the author of nearly 100 children's books. Her poetry has
been published in the U.S., Canada, the U.K., Japan, Romania, and
Australia, among others. Cathy and her husband, Doug Walker, own
Black Cat Press.

taking a nap
in the window the struggle
of a mosquito

in the clear dawn sky,
Haiku Canada Members' Anthology, 2009

honeymoon site
grandmother revisits
by herself

Into Our Words,
Haiku North America Anthology, 2009

My home is surrounded by rivers and mountains, a perfect setting to write Japanese poetry. Each day I try to translate my life experiences in some short poems. And what a joy when they are published!

Grant Savage and Ruby Spriggs

prone on the bridge,
our guide meaSures thE creek's dEpth
with his walking stick

wrought iron chairs
row upon row
on the college lawn

Michael Dudley is the author of fifteen poetry collections, a member
of the World Congress of Poets, and the father of three children.

so inviting
lips in the magazine

orange peels
the kids have come
and gone

André Duhaime vit en Outaouais. Il explore les formes poétiques d'origine japonaise depuis plus de trente ans. Il a reçu le Prix Canada-Japon 2008 pour le haibun *Marcher le silence* coécrit avec André Girard.

snow falling
on evergreens
her feathered hat

dad's gone for good
in the closet
she sits on his shoes

Award winning educator and author of ten poetry books for children and mainstream adult audiences. Drama consultant, storyteller, actor, television producer and performer for the CBC, CTV in Sudbury and the Rogers Cable network. Received Trailblazer Award from provincial arts organization Music and Film in Motion.

distant glimmer
of a beach fire—
autumn moonrise

Heron's Nest, April '02

in the park
motionless swings
moonlit

Ambrosia, spring '09 issue 3

Marje A. Dyck has had her short stories, articles, free verse, haiku, tanka, tanka sequences, haibun, and sumi-e paintings published in over seventy-five journals. Her books include *rectangle of light* (proof press, 1996), and *A Piece of the Moon* (Calisto Press, 2005).

kicking a white
            dandelion
blare of the noon siren

                                        bottle rockets II:1

after every
            passing car
spring peepers

David Elliott was born in Minneapolis in 1944, attended high school
in New Jersey, went to college in Vermont, grad school in upstate
New York, and teaches English at Keystone College in northeastern
Pennsylvania, where he has been writing and publishing haiku for
over 30 years.

draft resister
watching the ducks
fly south

Crossing Lines:
Poets Who Came to Canada
in the Vietnam War Era

cavern pool
tourists watching
blind fish

Foot Through the Ceiling

Chris Faiers, 'cricket' (b. Hamilton 1948-), entered haiku path 1968, meditating and publishing in Eric Amann's magazine, *Haiku*. Founding member Haiku Canada, Canadian Poetry Association. Founder Unfinished Monument Press, Main Street Library Readings, PurdyFests. Haibun/memoir *Eel Pie Dharma* 1990. 17 collections. Steward ZenRiver Gardens.

autumn moon—
alone in the hot tub
bought for his wife

country stroll
blackberries just beyond
the prick of barbed wire

Elizabeth is a retired English teacher. She teaches writing, literature
and haiku in a learning-in-retirement group, Renaissance Institute,
Notre Dame University of Maryland, where she first began writing
haiku. She is co-founder of the Haiku Poets of Central Maryland.

re-lacing
his old baseball glove
for his daughter

ambulance
two townhouses down—
days grow shorter

An Invertebrate Paleontologist, retired due to lung disease, he lives
in Sudbury, Ontario. Having written haiku poorly for 20 years, he is
a devoted student with a long way to go but one's who's beginning to
understand the true nature of the form.

strong wind from the east
each blade of grass belonging
to the other...

the gentle lift
of a curtain
Easter morning

Liz fenn lives and writes as a catholic solitary, currently from New
York State's Southern Tier.

slender icicle
vanishing in warm sunlight,
glistening droplets

poised, nose twitching
the hare stares at dogs barking
behind frosted glass

Having worked a forest fire lookout on a mountain ridge in Western
Alberta, Val continues to enjoy mountain hiking and camping.
Currently winding down her teaching career, Val lives in Edmonton
with her two Schnoodles, enjoying and appreciating each haiku mo-
ment life offers.

a howling wind
who knew I too would
miss the crows

Haiku Canada Newsletter
Spring 2004

in the spotlight
the flautist
and a moth

Haiku Canada Newsletter
Summer 2003

Visual artist and haiku poet, born in Toronto, Canada in 1926. Member of the Society of Canadian Artists, she exhibited paintings for over fifty years in southern Ontario, she is past Vice-President of Haiku Canada and co-founder of Haiku Deer Park.

my old cherry tree
    beneath its falling blossoms
        his last resting place

Sakura Award,
VCBF 2008

suddenly
    in the rain barrel, my face
        has no wrinkles

Fleeting Moments,
Bondi Studios, 2011

Gill Foss has been writing haiku since coming to Canada in 1970 and joined Ottawa KaDo at the first meeting. She has recently published *Fleeting Moments,* a chapbook of haiku, with Bondi Studios of Carleton Place.

summer campgrounds
a blues harmonica
starts up in the night

loosening leaves
the teacher sets her class
to silent reading

Alice Frampton is retired from childcare and lives in Seabeck, Washington, right on the beach where she grew up. She loves to kayak and swim, and she adores her new chihuahua. Four years ago she moved back from Canada to care for her mother.

on the teacher's desk
beside the box of kleenex
a first bunch of lilacs

autumn crows
undressing from the funeral
we make love

Marco Fraticelli has been writing haiku for over 35 years. For most of
that time he has served on the executive board of Haiku Canada.

frost at the window
a bowl of white rice
steaming

charcoal
    drawing the tree
        it was

Sandra Fuhringer served as President of Haiku Canada from 1982 to 1985. Among her accomplishments, she was the first prize winner of the inaugural 1998 Drevniok Award Contest. Her collection *The Tree It Was* (King's Road Press, 2002) appeared as part of the Hexagram Series.

wake up call
I cling to the remnants
of my dream

street busker's guitar
drowned out
by cell phones

I was introduced to haiku in my retirement, and appreciated the
guidance of the Deer Park Toronto group.

old hammock
a bowl of strawberries
on her stomach

Asahi Weekly Haiku Column,
Japan, 2009

summer's end
I pedal home
in the new darkness

Margot Gallant is an Ottawa-based haiku and lyric poet who has been writing both forms for the past decade. Her haiku has appeared in *Haiku Canada Review*, Kado Ottawa broadsheets and chapbooks, and once overseas in a Japanese newspaper, the *Asahi Weekly Haiku Column*.

not quite perfect,
the reflection of trees
in the lake

94th birthday—
the cake recipe yellow,
brittle with age

John Garrett grew up in the US near Boston and moved to British
Columbia in 1964. He has been dabbling in haiku since 1996 when he
semi-retired from a career as an ocean scientist. He is more interested
in the practice of haiku than in publication.

in her house
the fragrance
of walked-home flowers

between the clothesline
and the grey-green horizon
much left unsaid

Published in *The Haiku Canada Review, Bottle Rockets, Red Moon Anthology* and in local anthologies. She received an Honourable Mention and a Sakura Award with the Vancouver Cherry Blossom Festival Haiku Contest and had one haiku set to music and performed by members of the Vancouver Opera.

untended fish stall—
the lobsters
stir in their tanks

Modern Haiku 30.3,
1999

screensaver—
my icons scattered
around Stonehenge

frogpond 34.1,
2011

Barry George writes mostly about the nature and human nature in
and around Philadelphia, Pennsylvania, where he lives with his wife,
Heidi, and two cats. He gives haiku and tanka workshops, and teaches
English at Community College of Philadelphia.

cancer...
delicate curves
of the kidney bowl

days grow short
the paperboy one house
ahead of dusk

Shiki Monthly Kukai,
January 2008

Irene Golas has published haiku in a number of journals, including *Acorn, frogpond, Simply Haiku, The Heron's Nest* and *World Haiku Review.* Her poems have also appeared in *Carpe Diem: Canadian Anthology of Haiku* and several Red Moon Press anthologies. She lives in Sudbury, Ontario.

caterpillar
turning a leaf
into itself

Haiku Canada
Holographic Anthology, 2004

snow-laden evening
from branch to branch
the moon

Invisible Tea,
Bondi Studios, 2006

Ann is a former Vice-President of Haiku Canada, and for ten years
coordinated the Drevniok Award. She also writes for children and
paints. First inspired by Ryuho's haiku found in a school text: *I scooped
up the moon/ in my water bucket/ and spilled it on the grass.*

books balanced
the bones of take-out chicken
go back in the box

Presence #42,
September 2010

a blizzard outside
I want to believe
what the preacher says

The Heron's Nest,
December 2010

LeRoy Gorman lives in Napanee, Ontario. As well as writing, he edits
Haiku Canada Review and publishes poetry leaflets and postcards
under his *pawEpress* imprint. He is a member of the Writers' Union
of Canada, Haiku Society of America, and Life Member of Haiku
Canada.

Rio Dolce
Sunrise between volcanoes
Breaking the fast

Cedar waxwing flock
berry picking and pecking
—spring cackle

For four years now, Jeanne has been an active member of a bilingual poetry writing haiku group called Haiku Quebec. She is one of the authors of *Écris-moi un jardin,* a bilingual anthology of 230 haiku poems, published last year, describing The Van den Hende Gardens in Quebec City.

Michael Dylan Welch

In 2001, the Haiku Canada weekend was in Kingston, Ontario. I flew from California to Boston, and then carpooled to Kingston with Nicholaes Roosevelt. After our long drive, I remember stopping along the lakeshore in Kingston, less than a mile from the meeting facility. We needed to stretch our legs and unwind. Nick and I ended up skipping stones across the very calm lake water for nearly half an hour. It was foggy, so some of our stones skipped out of view into the fog. Somehow that shared moment of camaraderie captured the weekend for me, even though I also enjoyed giving a presentation on different ways to write haiku (about process and product), and the fact that Bruce Ross very kindly bought a cake to celebrate my birthday (on May 20, so always close to or during the Haiku Canada weekend).

For the 2005 Haiku Canada weekend, I carpooled from British Columbia to Lethbridge, Alberta with Alice Frampton and Vicki McCullough. We wrote rengay along the way (which included a quick side trip to Waterton Lakes National Park). At the conference I remember talking about the problem of pseudo-haiku (in the car I'd brought two boxes full of such books from my library), and giving a presentation on "Haikuholics Anonymous," which is now on my graceguts.com site. Haiku Canada meetings have inspired me to use anonymous workshops at other retreats, and also helped to inspire the Seabeck Haiku Getaway I started. In addition, the organization's practice of publishing Haiku Canada Sheets motivated me years ago to start creating my own haiku trifolds, which I've encouraged other people to make for such events as Haiku North America and other retreats. Haiku Canada has a rich tradition, one that has influenced hundreds of haiku poets across the continent—something to be proud of!

spring rain
dodging the puddles
I once ran to

coffeehouse clamour
the philosophy student
closes his text

Ottawa-based Alexander Halil searches for haiku in all aspects of his life. Inspired by his poet uncle, Ilyas Halil, he got started thanks to an introductory course taught by Terry Ann Carter. Other favourite poets include George Swede, Nick Virgilio and Alexis Rotella.

Father's watercolour—
how blue the lake
of my childhood

Asahi Shimbun English Web Ed.,
June 18, 2010

I lit the stove
a moth
flew out

Mainichi Daily News,
Dec. 11, 2010

John Hamley is a retired fisheries scientist and computer salesman, now playing amateur writer and forester in the woods of eastern Ontario. His haiku have been published in Canada and Japan.

after love
she traces the ferns
in the window's frost

Tracing the Fern,
HNA 2005 Anthology
Press Here

do I gather peonies
or do they gather me—
the summer garden

A Spray of Dogwood,
Haiku Canada conference, 2007

Penny Harter is widely published in journals and anthologies. Her most recent book is *Recycling Starlight*. A Dodge poet, she read at the 2010 Dodge Festival. She has won three fellowships from the NJSCA, the Mary Carolyn Davies Award from the PSA, and a VCCA fellowship.

each day
between the cedars
a rebuilt web

Haiku Canada Newsletter,
2006

after the rain
the cardinal's
cheerful whistle

Haiku Canada Newsletter,
2007

Introduced to haiku by Terry Ann Carter, Lois's poems have appeared in *Haiku Canada, Snapshot Press, Basho Festival* & others. Taught English to postgrads at Algonquin Tech. In Choral Society; Mendelssohn & Church Choir, Germany. Other interests: pastel portraits & those grandkids.

after her swim
sunlight flies everywhere
as she shakes her hair

my lover's footprints
once so deep in the snow   now
barely visible

Ko Spring, 2005

Active and healthy for forty-eight years, I then suffered a series of
debilitating illnesses which I've dealt with positively for twenty-three
years. My book, *Wing to Wing: Inspirations for Dealing with Life's
Adversities,* published last year, has sold 600 copies and includes over
forty haiku.

up-drafted pages
crinkled by wind and rain
mulching my garden

throat duets in
inuktituk—blasts, blizzards, winds
howling in dissonance

The Envoy, March 2011,
pp. 6-7

Sterling Haynes is an octogenarian who writes poetry, humorous short stories and haiku. His latest book, *Wake Up Call: tales from a frontier doctor,* published by Caitlin/Harbour Press is selling well. His first book, *Bloody Practice,* was a BC bestseller.

flea market closes
memories tossed
into dumpsters

painter scumbles
sharp edges into soft
when does grieving stop?

Helen Herr may be known as a mother, piano teacher, ordained
minister, writer and artist. Now retired in Watrous, Saskatchewan, she
longs for a simpler life. That is why writing various forms of haiku is
an ideal fit.

(1938-2008)

through the muck
and rubbish of this world ...
forsythia

where builders
trampled all last fall
the first gold crocus

William J. Higginson is best known for *The Haiku Handbook, Haiku Seasons,* and *Haiku World*—and for his own poems and haiku, as well as translations, reviews, and essays he offered on the worldwide web. He held awards from the Witter Bynner Foundation, the NJSCA, and the HSA.

Penny Harter

Gosh, my strongest memories about Bill at Haiku Canada are from the last Haiku Canada weekend we attended together, when we decided we just wanted to be observers and not offer any workshops. That was the weekend he took so many photos and then created a wonderful photo-montage of the entire event, with commentary. I remember how enthusiastic he was about doing that—and so excited about how it came together when he worked on it afterward at home. I think it's still in your archives, somewhere. And I remember his wanting to photograph the moon out the window during the late-night renku session.

I have more foggy memories of a long ago weekend at Aylmer—maybe Bill was part of that big argument Grant refers to, since I remember a meeting when Bill was being somewhat autocratic—that was before I mellowed him some :)—and voices were raised. I don't remember with whom the "discussion" was—I do remember giant mosquitoes on the river bank :)!

after the rain...
the red-wing claiming
his own warm puddle

my upturned face
braving the hail
... snowgeese

As far back as I can remember, I read and wrote poetry. Before discovering haiku, I found myself naturally drawn to short, concise forms, starting with Korean Sijo. This has informed my artwork, which is fine and realistic. Poetry defines me. It is my oxygen.

Dorothy Howard

the darkening snow clouds
an apple left on the tree
    shivering

a ladybug
    struggles to climb
        the berry juice jar

Kimiko Horne: Born in Japan, moved to Scotland and in 1964 immigrated to Canada. Member Haiku Canada and Kaitei (Japan). Publication, *in the mist* (2010), features 300 Haiku in English and Japanese. Retired in 2000 from teaching Japanese at Brock University. Resident of St. Catharines, Ontario.

fog.
sitting here
without the mountains

distant thunder—
the dog's toenails click
against the linoleum

Gary Hotham has been writing and publishing haiku since the 1960s in various literary magazines and journals and chapbooks. His first major collection, *Breath Marks: Haiku to Read in the Dark,* was published in 1999 and his most recent collection, *Spilled Milk: Haiku Destinies,* in 2010.

arrivant en ville par l'autoroute spaghetti　　tout à coup
　　trop chaud

spaghetti-way into the city　　suddenly too hot

Dorothy Howard, ancienne présidente de Haïku Canada et son archiviste actuelle est une des directrices de *casse-pieds*, la revue du poème bref, dans sa dernière année de parution. En somme, elle va prendre le temps de vivre un peu, avec les haïkus qu'elle aime entre autres.

the way passing cars
        become wind in the pines
                beside the river

    you stand
              to watch the sunrise
    i watch it
             shine on you

Marshall Hryciuk was President of Haiku Canada from 1990 until 1998. He writes and publishes poetry while residing in Toronto with his beautiful wife, the poet Karen Sohne.

green maple leaves
in bonsai
turning to red

applause
from a group of veiled women
for a skater

Liette Janelle is from Boucherville, Quebec. Ex secretary for Standard
Life and MCSC English Dept. Seven years of haiku. Member of HC,
AFH, HI and Gusts. Winner in French and English, *Mainichi Journal*'s
14th contest, international section 2010. Honourable mention in
Torino and Montpellier, France.

farm foreclosure
bees continue to work
the flower bed

in the clear dawn sky:
Haiku Canada Members' Anthology
2009

meditation hall
linguist has six languages
to silence

Harvey Jenkins lives on Vancouver Island. He has received Honourable Mentions for his haiku in the Vancouver Cherry Blossom Festival and the Thunder Bay International Fine Arts Association contest. His haiku have appeared in the last three editions of the *Haiku Canada Members' Anthology*.

Hans Jongman and anne mckay

on my way home
chasing the sun
going down

trails of ivy
the pendulum swings
in the watchmaker's shop

Hans Jongman. Born in Holland in 1950. Youngest crew member on the liner "Statendam" on its 1966 "Around the World Tour." Also worked the Rotterdam-NewYork run before the demise of trans-Atlantic crossings in the late 1960s. Immigrated to Canada in 1969... by air.

he ties one hole
to another—fisherman
mending his nets

> *New Kid on the Block*:
> haiku and senryu

graveside ceremony
burial urn
warm in her hands

> *New Kid on the Block*:
> haiku and senryu

Jean, a retired nurse, comes from an Alberta farming background.
After years of writing rhymed and free verse, as well as short stories,
she began writing haiku and related poetry in 1987. Her work appears
in a number of anthologies and five published books of poetry.

let me say
good night to you
spring's embrace

your lips obey
drawing my lips
cherry blossom rain

Makiko Kageura. Born in 1972 in Ehime, Japan. M.A. in English and American Literature, Sophia University, Tokyo. Student at Niagara College. Began to write haiku in 2008. Recipient of a prize at the 12th annual Mainichi Haiku Contest. Member of WHA, HSA and Haiku Canada.

yoga class
we sit quietly together
after the hurricane

World Haiku Review

Louisiana
New Orleans estate sale
statue of Robert E. Lee

Howard Lee Kilby served as secretary of the Haiku Society of America, 1999-2002. He is native to Hot Springs National Park, Arkansas. hkilby@hotmail.com

Philomene Kocher listens to a
presentation in 2004.

rose hips and roses and buds
on the same bush
August evening

frogpond XXIV. 1,
2001

only by its shadow
seeing the white hair
on the blank page

Haiku Canada Sheet
1999

Philomene Kocher lives in Kingston, Ontario. She began writing haiku in 1991 and tanka in 2001, and her poetry has appeared in Canada, the United States and Japan. She served as secretary for Haiku Canada from 1998 to 2010.

Sushi chef
goldfish in the pond
dart away

Modern Haiku, 1988

methodical husband—
on his list of chores, she finds
her name

frogpond, 1990

Krumins has published one collection, *This Day's New Face* (Haiku Canada Sheet, 1993). Her work has also appeared in *frogpond, Inkstone, Modern Haiku,* etc. and a number of anthologies. She was past assistant editor of *frogpond* and lives in Toronto.

walking walking—
I leave
myself behind

icy cold
a poinsettia
warms the room

Mr. Kusmiss is a retired computer scientist. He attended Brown University and Syracuse University and worked for IBM and MITRE. He also taught Computer Science at the University of Texas, UNH, Dartmouth and Saint Anselm College. Mr. Kusmiss currently resides in Sanbornton, New Hampshire.

ELIZABETH SEARLE LAMB
(1917-2005)

sky darkening moon brightening crickets

RawNerVZ Essentials,
2002

he prunes the juniper
bright blue berries falling
beneath the wind chimes

Beyond Spring Rain:
Members' Anthology,
2002

Early president of the Haiku Society of America, and editor of *frogpond* for eight years, her haiku have been widely published and translated, won numerous awards, and appeared frequently in international, as well as Canadian, anthologies.

new moon
a howling wind drowns out
the house crickets

World Haiku Review #6-3,
May 2008,
Best 10 Honorable Mention

...and more rain
the motel parking lot full
of tent trailers

Concise Delight, 2,
Winter 2009

Catherine J.S. Lee lives and writes on a Maine island near Canada. Her haiku and senryu appear in a variety of print and online journals. *All That Remains,* her collection, won the 2010 Turtle Light Press Haiku Chapbook Competition and was published in April 2011.

autumn nightfall
the widow next door
draws her shades

departing geese—
my tongue travels
the length of his belly

Angela Leuck is the author of ten poetry collections and has edited
numerous anthologies. She is currently at work on *Haiku Teen: A
Contemporary Anthology*.

on the way
to the Zen garden
dog dung

jigsaw puzzle:
group-home kids piece together
"American Dream"

                                    (American Dream is FX Schmid's
                                award-winning 750-piece jigsaw puzzle)

Chen-ou Liu was born in Taiwan and emigrated to Canada in 2002.
Featured in *A New Resonance 7*, he is the author of *Following the Moon
to the Maple Land*, the First Prize winner of the Spring 2011 Haiku Pix
Chapbook Contest.

mountain pass
the only thing we see clearly—
fog

Me and You:
Haiku of Love and Loss,
November, 2011

moving day
only the memories
left behind

Fascination with Asian art, philosophy and poetry as a teenager eventually led me to a serious pursuit of learning Asian brush painting and writing haiku. I'm grateful to members of KaDo Ottawa for their encouragement and support of my journey along this path.

summer cottage—
last year's mosquitoes
still on the wall

Samoborski Susreti,
Croatia, 2007

lilac in full bloom—
bees bumping
into bees

Tiny Words,
2006-07-14

Carole MacRury resides in Point Roberts, Washington. Her poems have received numerous awards and been published worldwide. She is affiliated with the VCBF Haiku Invitational as past judge and workshop leader of Haiku Garden. Her first book, *In the Company of Crows,* was published in 2008.

last rites
between my palms
the setting sun

night wind
the ornamental grass
nudges the moon

Terra Martin's poetry has been published in *Amaze, American Tanka, Asahi Shimbun, Atlas Poetica, Eucalypt, Gusts, Lynx, Modern English Tanka, Ribbons, Simply Haiku, Landfall* and *Streetlights*.

done for the day
my dad brings to supper
the smell of turned earth

The Heron's Nest 8.3,
2006

above the trees
a mountain has melted
into haze

Michael McClintock lives in Clovis and Los Angeles, California. He has been writing and editing haiku, haibun, tanka, and related poetry since the 1960s and is a regular contributor of essays, criticism, and reviews to specialist journals and magazines devoted to the short poem.

red light—
zigzagging through traffic
a butterfly

Haiku Canada Newsletter,
June, 2005

a woodlouse
treks the concrete floor—
funeral tea

Vicki McCullough is the BC (pacifi-kana) regional coordinator for
Haiku Canada. She was a founding co-organizer of the Vancouver
Cherry Blossom Festival Haiku Invitational in 2006 and continues
to organize festival haiku events. A freelance editor, writer, and
standardized-patient actor, she resides in Vancouver.

autumn leaves—
in the rummage box
his cold shoes

Haiku Canada
Members' Anthology,
2008

the train's whistle—
for a moment long grass
blowing west

Leanne McIntosh lives in Nanaimo, BC. Her poems have appeared in numerous journals and chapbooks. Two books of poetry, *The Sound the Sun Makes* and *Liminal Space,* were published by Oolichan Books. She is currently working on a third collection of poems titled, *The Habit of Being.*

132

ANNE MCKAY
(1932-2003)

pinning sheets in the hot morning
the clean taut line
            of her stretching

RawNerVZ Essentials,
2002

a child rolls a hoop into autumn

RN X. 2,
2005

anne mckay published fourteen books of haiku, renga, and tanka,
among them, *a cappella*. Her soft, romantic way of writing, all in lower
case, influenced many other poets.

Forgetting her name
but not her perfume
wisteria

> *Troubadour Ginyu,*
> *Vol. 14,* ed. Ban'ya Natsuishi,
> Saitama: Japan, 2002

New surname
carved deeply into
summerwood

Toronto-born David McMurray summers at Maple Lake in the
Algonquin Highlands, authors *Asahi Haikuist Network* www.asahi.
com/english/haiku, is professor of international haiku at The Inter-
national University of Kagoshima and leads the Asahi Culture Centre
Haiku in English correspondence course in Tokyo.

young girls
run to catch the
tram—wet snow

o god, how i miss
the pickled cabbage today
—very cold

I was born in Zagreb, Croatia in 1953 and have studied law, philosophy
and Waldorf/Steiner education in Zagreb, Belgrade, Stuttgart, Vienna,
Konstanz and Turku. I have a wife and three daughters and have pub-
lished more than hundred haiku in English. I live in Vienna.

George Swede, Margaret Saunders,
LeRoy Gorman and Marshall Hryciuk

RAFFAEL DE GRUTTOLA

There are so many memorable moments during the Haiku Canada Weekends over the years. I've also worked closely with LeRoy Gorman with our mutual interest in concrete haiku and renku. I've done some wonderful renku over the Net with Claudia Radmore and Dorothy Howard that appeared in Dorothy's *RawNerVS* magazines. I'm also in communication with Marshall Hryciuk and Nick Avis in our mutual interests in the experimental nature of the Japanese poetic forms.

Through Marshall I met bpNichol's widow and have maintained a correspondence with her over the years. Another fine artist I met through all my Canadian friends was jwcurry, an experimental visual artist who is one of the finest artists I believe working today. It was through the bpNichol connection that I was able to have some experimental work published by Steve McCaffery, one of the legendary Four Horsemen poets of the Toronto Research Group.

And of course Terry Ann Carter in our trip to Japan and connection with Cambridge, Ma. And last but not least, Marco Fraticelli, without whom, I wouldn't have anyone to argue with.

creeping along
last year's flower stalk
a golden snail

Haiku Canada Members' Anthology,
2009

winter dawn
black and white
the red barn

Haiku Canada Sheet
Fundy Shores
June, 2001

Born in rural British Columbia, Ruth-Ann Mitchell exchanged one
coast for the other in 1979 and currently lives near the Bay of Fundy.
Her most recent creative endeavours are in the field of hand made
books, some of which incorporate her haiku.

- 3 word 3 line haiku

autumn
leaves
winter

deep winter—
almost not noticing the star
alone in the night

Ruth Mittelholtz is inspired by the forests, fens and limestone escarpment lands of Bruce County, Ontario. Her haiga have been published online at *Daily Haiga* and *Modern Haiga*. She has made several handbound collections of her haiku and haiga.

I remove the label
from another empty jar
                    deep winter

winter sunset
a door opens
inside the mirror

Emiko Miyashita (1954-) was born in Fukushima, Japan. Her favorite
music is cicada songs in summer and cricket songs in autumn. She
writes haiku in both Japanese and English. A great fan of illy issimo
and loves it black.

Sunday morning walk -
the smell of bacon
from every other house

bottle rockets
9. 2

she patiently
waits in line -
one finger nail at a time

frogpond,
32. 2

Mike Montreuil lives in Ottawa, Ontario with his family and a trio of
cats. When not watching hockey, he can be found at one of the many
coffee shops in Ottawa.

fall sunshine
the copier warms up
in the library

Modern Haiku, 42.1,
Winter-Spring 2011

a train whistles
from the other side of town
autumn wind

frogpond, 31.2,
Spring/Summer 2008

Lenard D. Moore teaches at Mount Olive College, where he directs
the literary festival and advises *The Trojan Voices.* He is author of
A Temple Looming, and other books. He is recipient of The Haiku
Museum of Tokyo Award (1983, 1994 and 2003), among others.

field of hay bales
and their shadows
the hawk's wingspan

About the Blue Moon

passion play
I watch the crucifixion
through binoculars

About the Blue Moon

Joanne Morcom is a poet, social worker and a "living book" library
volunteer who lives in Calgary, Alberta. Her latest poetry book, *About
the Blue Moon*, is available from Inkling Press/Magpie Productions in
Edmonton, Alberta.

in spring sunlight
a block of sugar in my tea
getting out of shape

singing a capella
winter moonlight
on the lake

Makoto Nakanishi is a professor at Ehime University, Faculty of Education, in Japan. His study includes literacy education in elementary and secondary schools. His main focus is how to teach haiku to elementary school children.

In that ugly ditch
over by the railway tracks,
nine kinds of wildflowers.

No birds.
But a single white feather
floats to the ground.

Larry Neily, a Nova Scotian living in Ottawa, a birder who works
in geomatics/remote sensing, has tinkered with haiku since being
introduced to them by his late wife Marianne Bluger at HC1990. He
and new wife Antoinette have a winter home in Arizona.

under the umbrella
a child reaches
for the rain

Haiku Canada Review
2. 1, Feb. 2008

through the windows
of the sway-backed barn
city lights

Haiku Canada Members' Anthology,
2010

For me haiku has been a form of expression tied to meditation and focus. As a visual artist sometimes I find I am in a dilemma between words and vision, but ultimately the gift is the moment itself, even if it passes unrecorded.

rustling leaves
the scent of gardenia
on my cat's fur

The Heron's Nest,
IX. 3, 2007

rusty wheelbarrow—
a red leaf floats
in rainwater

White Lotus,
8, 2009

Nancy Nitrio began writing haiku in 2007 and has been published in various paper and online journals/anthologies in the USA and internationally. She lives in the Sacramento area of California with her husband and five cats. She also enjoys the practice of ikebana and origami.

blue christmas lights
on the solitary house
ash wednesday

Haiku Canada Members' Anthology,
2011

scent of mussels still
on my fingers
and the idea of your tongue

forthcoming in the
Nietzsche's Brolly anthology,
Do Not Write In This Space,
August 2012, ed. Marshall Hryciuk

Melanie Noll started exploring haiku and related forms in 2001. Her poetic focus is on renku and urban senryu. When she attended the 25th anniversary Haiku Canada Weekend at Glendon College she felt like she had found family and has not turned back.

knee-deep snow
covers the orchard
one apple left to freeze

a lone sparrow flits
from pillar to pillar
in the church

Michael O. Nowlan of Oromocto, NB, has been teacher and writer
for 50 years. He first wrote haiku about 15 years ago and is now com-
mitted to the form. He considers his honorary Doctor of Letters de-
gree for contribution to education, writing, and philately his special
accomplishment.

up bright and early
arranging flowers
to look unarranged

porch rocker empty
the blue cedar's shadow
slowly climbs up the steps

H. F. (Tom) Noyes was the 2007–2008 honorary curator of the
American Haiku Archives at the California State Library in Sacra-
mento. Noyes's haiku was published worldwide; he is well known for
his 'favourite haiku' comments in haiku journals.

potter's wheel
inside and out the shape
of her clay

South by Southeast, 3.3

August moon
the cricket throb
in me too

Basho Festival Dedicatory Anthology,
1996

Marian Olson is the author of four books of poetry, among them *Desert Hours,* which won first place in the 2008 Merit Book Awards and was a finalist in the 2008 New Mexico Book Awards.

midwinter sermon
hardened drops of varnish
on the pews

Cascade No. 1
Washington Poets Association, 2007

sugar maple
the fingerless gloves
of the fiddler

The 2007 Betty Drevniok Award broadsheet,
2008

Roland Packer lives in Hamilton, Ontario teaching piano, music
theory and composition as well as playing hammered dulcimer in a
duo called The Playford Players. He is one of the featured haiku poets
in *A New Resonance 6* published by Red Moon Press in 2009.

GRANT SAVAGE

It was late at night. Perhaps midnight, Saturday. The haiku weekend was going well. My ride wanted to stay for several more hours, so I went out to the meadow at the back of *le monastère*, planning to contemplate.

Time passed. The night got colder. Clouds went by. And more clouds.

Startled by a killdeer's cry, I came to, wondering if my ride might have left. I stretched, then went in, where I was instantly confronted by tired, chastened people, who looked as if they'd bitten into a lemon.

"Why are you looking at me like that?" I asked.

"Where have you been?" someone queried.

Turned out I'd missed the fight. One VIP had suddenly lit into the partner of another VIP, who leapt to his partner's defence. Apparently it didn't take long for everyone to find offence or to be the best defence.

I looked around at the piled up cases of empties, stroked my beard, and answered, "Meditating under the moon of course."

Tendrils of grapevine,
hang low
a lone shadow.

Cicadas rasp,
under the noon sun
silence louder still.

Kamal Parmar's genre is poetry as well as creative non-fiction. She has
published a few books. She has had her haiku as well as haibun poems
published in US and Canadian anthologies and in online journals.
She is currently in the process of writing haiga poems.

trimming tall bamboo,
the morning moon
and fog leaving

I search for the way
with map and wind—
thistledown

Born Anchorage, 1953. Graduated Santa Cruz, 1975—followed by 6 ½ years of formal zen practice. Haiku began to be published, 1986. Team translations: 8,000 contemporary haiku with Sakuzô Takada; also 1,400 Shinto waka, and one volume Shinto prose with Hiroaki Narita. Employed as a nurseryman.

Marco Fraticelli and LeRoy Gorman

old swimming hole
willow branches
test the water

Canadian Author & Bookman

washing her kittens
each stroke of her tongue
pushing them away

Inkstone

Born in England, and Canadian by choice, Mary Partridge was a long-time member of the Hamilton Haiku Workshop. Widely published, Mary now makes her home in northern Ontario.

cloudless sky—
I no longer know
where to look

the boat
at the very end of the wharf—
and two moons

HNA Anthology,
August 2009

Self-taught poet, Luce Pelletier writes free-form poetry, haiku and
haibun (French and English). Her poems can be found in a number
of collections, magazines, and self-published works. She has received
honourable mentions in various contests including Mainichi,
Genkissu, Kikakuza and Radio-Canada Literary Awards.

all fog
all frost
glitter*fall*

Haiku Canada Newsletter,
XIX. 3, 2006
outside back cover

I lift my eyes
to the sky
                 call of the cranes

June 20, 1985. I was looking out at our patch of rural Alberta,
wondering what to do, with husband away and children in bed, when
a deer appeared at sunset. The threads of my life converged in that
moment, and I wrote my first poem.

a glacier's wind
the sour taste
of sorrel

frogpond,
Summer 2009

catching my breath
the mountains
beneath me

Wisteria,
January, 2009

Linda Pilarski has lived in the USA, Australia and Canada. With her notebook and camera, she has hiked in wild and beautiful places on all seven continents. Her haiku and haiga have appeared in print and online. She is editor of the online journal *DailyHaiga*.

easter morning
the tilted heads
of daffodils

Huge Blue,
Leaf Press, 2009

biting wind
the sheep's face
hidden in fleece

paper wasp
15. 3, 2009

Patrick M. Pilarski is the author of *Huge Blue* (Leaf Press, 2009) and two chapbooks. His work has appeared in journals and anthologies across North America, Europe, Australia, and Japan. Patrick is co-editor of *DailyHaiku,* and poetry editor for *DailyHaiga.* He lives in Edmonton.

the hawk
being eaten
by fog

frosty porch
sack of corn cobs
and their worms

Pearl Pirie has been fortunate enough to be a member of KaDo
Ottawa for a few years. She writes various forms. Her author site is at
www.pearlpirie.com

mother's day
toddler
picking dandelions

first starling
I work on
my income tax

Age 87, happy to breathe. Challenge others to share happiness being
alive and still searching the right words for love. English my second
language. Frustrating choices.

spring evening
playing my piano
for all the street to hear

Betty Drevniok Award,
Hon. Mention, 2010

a winter blizzard
I turn my calendar
to cherry blossoms

Best Canadian Poem,
Haiku Invitational, 2008

Marilyn Potter's poetry has appeared in *Prism international, Room, American Tanka, Ribbons, The Heron's Nest,* and *Take Five: Best Contemporary Tanka Vol. 2.* Marilyn has won the Betty Drevniok Award, the Toronto Art Bar Discovery Night, and Best Canadian Poem in the Haiku Invitational.

always a few steps
ahead of me
grasshopper

Hon. Mention, Kaji Aso Studio,
International Haiku Competition, 2007

winter
my toenails
growing longer

Haiku Canada Review,
3. 2, 2009

Nancy Prasad, Toronto ON, graduated Queen's University (B.A.,
English and Psychology). Poems and essays were aired on CBC Radio;
short stories and poetry published for adults and children. Awards:
Betty Drevniok Award, Second Prize (2004); Kaji Aso International
Haiku Competition, Honourable Mention (2006 & 2007).

first snow...
silently in the darkness
flakes circling the lamp

Windchimes 10

August lull
entranced I had forgotten
the cricket

Windchimes 10

Well known as an artist, her interest in Japanese graphics drew her to
haiku. Often illustrating her haiku, Pratt is credited for *Haiku*, the first
English haiku book published in Canada after the war.

gathering storm
the scent of lavender
across the fence

NZPS Haiku Contest,
2nd Place, 2010

afternoon stillness
the sound of a lawnmower
across the valley

Patricia is co-editor of *Kokako* and reviews editor of *Takahe*. She will be reviews editor of *Haibun Today* from 2012. Patricia has interviewed poets and editors for *Takahe* and other journals. She was one of the readers for the *Take Five Anthologies,* 2008-2011. She lives in New Zealand.

geese in flight
their outstretched necks
and mine

paper wasp,
autumn 2007

end of summer
the goldfish swims under
a floating leaf

Hermitage, II.1

Originally from California, I've lived over half my life in the North Carolina mountains (USA). Retired from a social work career with the Eastern Band of Cherokees, I enjoy the simple life now. My work has appeared in a variety of national and international journals.

In Delhi
with a hand clap
a cloud of pigeons

à Delhi
en frappant des mains
un nuage de pigeons

I'm a retired French Immersion teacher from Calgary, Alberta. With the help of my daughter Lynn Del Castilho, I have published six haiku chapbooks for a fund raiser for Development and Peace. The last two were bilingual.

wheelbarrow
filled with manure
my mind is made up

anniversary
a spider web
in the knitting

Carolyne Rohrig can't explain it, but she's published in the United States, Canada, England, Ireland and Japan, and has won numerous awards and other honours. Her favourite part of the writing process is the *aha!* moment she herself experiences when reviewing a finished haiku.

Terry Ann Carter

One of my favourite Haiku Canada memories occurred at the 2001 Haiku Canada Weekend in Kingston, when Claudia Coutu Radmore and I stole some gorgeous crab apple branches from trees at the entrance of Queen's University, for our presentations on Women of the Heian Court and Chiyo-ni (respectively). Under the cover of night, we snuck into the entrance area with large cutters; we wanted to arrange our podium with blossoms, pink silk (to honour the women) and a large stone to anchor our thoughts. I'm not sure if the aha came at the moment of crack! or the moment of bliss when we first surveyed the room where we were to speak.

(The memory became even more dear when I learned that those trees have all been removed in favour of a large cement entranceway to the University.)

evening
the maple lays down
its shadow

> *Modern Haiku,*
> 40.3, 2009

autumn
unleaving...
leaves

> *Haiku Canada Review*
> 3.2, 2009

Michele Root-Bernstein appears in a number of North American haiku journals. She also has a selection of poems in *A New Resonance 6*. When she isn't thinking and composing haiku, she studies, writes and blogs on creative imagination and the invention of imaginary worlds.

t'ai chi studio
different coloured shoes
on every shelf

a static spark
and into the dark room
the winter moon

Bruce Ross was born in Hamilton, Ontario and resides in Hampden,
Maine with his wife Astrid. Bruce is the editor of *Haiku Moment: An
Anthology of Contemporary North American Haiku* and author of *How
to Haiku: A Writer's Guide to Haiku and Related Forms*.

white angora
on his navy jacket
last dance

———

Me and You, haiku of love and loss,
KaDo Ottawa, 2010

full moon
blue trees on snow
and my shadow

Shape Shifting,
Haiku Canada Members' Anthology,
2010

A contemporary lyric poet from Gatineau, Quebec, in 2007 Sheila began exploring Japanese writing forms. Her haiku and haibun have been published online and in print in *Contemporary Haibun #10, Shamrock,* and several broadsheets, chapbooks, reviews and anthologies. Sheila is a member of KaDo Ottawa and Haiku Canada.

ancient walls
on the ground...
a broken eggshell

rough cobblestone streets
softened by rows of orange trees

A native Calgarian and novice haiku poet, Colleen seeks inspiration
from the views outside her windows. The Rocky Mountains, prairie
grasslands and nature are always changing, and coming up with fresh
ideas is often a challenge.

tender saplings
in the breeze—
first ballet recital

foggy morning—
walking out the door
I disappear

Sylvia Santiago has ridden public transport in London (UK), walked
with wolves in Golden, visited a voodoo priestess in New Orleans,
and given readings with the Magpie Haiku Poets in Calgary. The
readings made her the most nervous.

MARGARET SAUNDERS
(1926-2005)

Final goodbye
lost
in the ship's horn

Nearing our destination
we pick up
a fresh flock of gulls

Margaret Saunders was born in Scotland. She was the editor and publisher of *Wee Giant* and *Daybreak* magazines. Her own books include *Snapdragons* and *Bridging the Gap*.

apples in bud
a white lie
about her complexion

The Heron's Nest
X.2

steep trail
i mistake grouse drumming
for my heartbeat

RAW NerVZ
VIII.1

Grant Savage, poet and nature photographer from Ottawa, writes a variety of Japanese forms. He's edited tanka and haiku books, and is author of *Their White With Them*, Bondi Studios, 2006; *Finding a Breeze*, King's Road Press, 2009; *The Swan's Wings* (renku with Ruby Spriggs), Ground Hog Press, 1994.

this finch
    with a yellow head
    grey clouds roll in from the west

the caterpillars are all white
    heavy snow this winter

Influenced by Chinese nature poetry, Rich (Irish/US) writes haiku, senryu, renku & haibun. Some poems are translated into Romanian, Navajo, Irish and Italian. In 2004 Mellen Poetry Press published *Adirondack Haiku: Kayaking in Fog*. Rich sails, kayaks, & cycles; lives where the Adirondack Mountains reach Lake Champlain.

harvest moon
grandpa's bedside clock
never so loud

creeping
into the green sumac
red sumac

Called "imagist/humourist" by lyric poet Marianne Bluger, Guy's
poems have earned prize recognition in USA, Japan and Canada and
publication in seven countries. He began writing with a straight pen
and inkwell. It offered time to think between words. He still does...
he thinks.

HANS JONGMAN:
REMEMBERING SHAUNT BASMAJIAN (1950-1990)

In the spring of 1989, Shaunt and I drove down to Aylmer, Quebec to attend the May '89 Haiku Canada Weekend held at *le monastère*.

During the 400 km we had ample time to chitchat. "I've had many jobs...all to support my writing," he told me. He talked about the time he was robbed and stabbed to within an inch of his life while driving a Toronto cab, and as a result was now on medication. No longer was he able to enjoy alcohol. When I asked him what he missed most he answered, "A beer!" Affectionately I called him "Mr. Bluesman."

He told me about his father's hope for an independent homeland Armenia. That passion he shared with his son, passion so essential to a bluesman.

When Shaunt recited his poetry it was a total experience, an emotional roller-coaster ride, articulate and with gusto. During one of our conversations, the subject of "rejection" came up. I meant "rejection" like in a publisher's rejection slip. Shaunt however took it to be a rejection from a new lover. As our friend Ted Plantos remarked in his poem, *A Class Production*, "Hurt was another of his names." Shaunt said that he has had so many rejections from publishers that these rejection slips would be in themselves interesting reading, and that he had enough material for a 48 page book. Shaunt was always thinking of another book. PS: His 1987 *Biased Analogies*, Anthos Books, counts exactly 48 pages.

so small and far away
the full moon
without you

ever since I was a child
the moon
following me home

Karen is from Long Island, New York. She's lived in Toronto with
her husband, Marshall Hryciuk, since 1999. She's only nice when she
feels like it.

182

RUBY SPRIGGS
(1929–2001)

midwinter
dried leaf arrangement
falling apart

moment of birth   new shadow

Ruby was born in Leicester, England, and moved to Canada in the late
fifties. She has four children. Dancer, singer, artist, editor, and widely
published poet, her three chapbooks are *Sun Shadow Moon Shadow*,
The Swan's Wings (with Grant Savage) and *Switching off the Shadows*.

the circle
of the winging hawk
tightens to a dot

Dance of Light,
maplebud press, 1995

last patch of snow
a small black spider
lowers into it

frogpond,
XIII.1,1990

Elizabeth St Jacques has authored four haiku books, including *Dance of Light* which earned the 1995 Haiku Society of America Award. Published internationally since the 1960s, her work has earned numerous awards. She has also served as haiku columnist, judge, editor, and publisher.

Betty Drevniok and George Swede

for the fat green frog
crouched on the log
time is flies

Tell-Tale Feathers,
Fiddlehead Poetry Books, 1978

leaving my loneliness   inside her

Cicada, 1979

Swede's two latest collections were published in 2010 by Edmonton's Inkling Press: *Joy In Me Still* (haiku), and *White Thoughts, Blue Mind* (tanka). He is the co-founder of Haiku Canada and past editor of *frogpond: Journal of the Haiku Society of America.*

entre ciel et terre
je me berce dans le hamac
entre prunes et poires

Regards de femmes,
AFH 2008.

pleine lune
toute la nuit, je rêve
de chapeaux

Magnapoets 7,
janvier 2011

Originaire d'Allemagne, vit à Montréal. Écrit des haïkus, renkus et tankas depuis 2005. Récipiendaire, avec Huguette Ducharme, du Prix Haïku 2011 de l'APH pour *Quelques grains de riz.* Première place du 5e kukai allemand (mai 2011). Codirection de l'anthologie bilingue *Montréal* (Kingsroad Press, 2010). mohe.xanga.com

earthquake
a cherry blossom
turns white

tremblement de terre
une fleur de cerisier
pâlit

Jessica Tremblay currently lives in Vancouver BC where she creates a weekly haiku comic called *Old Pond* (oldpond.voila.net). As a winner of Best BC Poem of the Vancouver Cherry Blossom Festival Haiku Invitational 2008, her poem was sculpted in a stone at the VanDusen botanical garden.

writer's block—
the tap tap tap of rain
on the skylight

Wednesday Haiku,
Issa's Untidy Hut,
Feb. 16, 2011

thinking deeply...
the stone I throw
fails to skip

Charles Trumbull is past president of the Haiku Society of America and current editor of *Modern Haiku*. He lives in Santa Fe, NM.

bazaar in Turkey
a vendor tells me
the soul weighs 13 grams

on the road
a rain-soaked pizza box
a dead seagull

Born in Germany, lived in Japan from 1970 to 2001, now resides in
Vancouver, Canada. Has been widely published in English newspapers
in Japan and Haiku International. Was runner-up in several contests
and won 1ˢᵗ prize in the 3ʳᵈ Mainichi International contest in 1999.

spring sun on the sill
    and in the pine cone's
        empty spaces

Modern Haiku, 10.3,
1979

the parsnip seeds:
I was about to plant them
when the wind blew

frogpond, XIII.1,
1990

Born 1929 in France, Russian parents. Haiku helps hone my English. The words 'ava kar' took meaning for more than pronunciation when I found they can mean 'word work' in some languages. Lived in America 35 years, in Canada since 1975, haiku since 1978.

Philomene Kocher

When Nick Avis was President, he encouraged poets to participate in the Open Reading at the Haiku Canada Weekends. He said that part of being a poet was sharing your work with an audience, and it would be easier to practise in front of others who already loved haiku. A workshop at the 2003 conference in Ottawa, "The Poetry of Performance," was facilitated by Ann Patteson who is a singing teacher. She reinforced that voice includes our speaking voice as well as the voice that finds expression in our haiku. I find it fascinating that after hearing someone read their work out loud, I can hear an echo of their voice when I read their work in print: a kind of haiku resonance.

JOCELYNE VILLENEUVE
(1941-1988)

Couleurs de l'été
mêlées aux cris d'un enfant
qui n'est pas le mien...

Colours of summer
and the cries of a child
that is not mine...

Jocelyne Villeneuve was born in Val d'Or, Quebec. She published a novel, poetry and prose for adults and children, as well as haiku in English and in French.

yet one more haiku
on cherry blossom. Are there
really new things to say?

end of summer
pinned to the park notice-board
a bikini top

Drevniok Award, 2011,
Honourable mention

Naomi Beth Wakan's books include: *Haiku: one breath poetry* (Heian International); *Segues; Late Bloomer: on writing later in life; Compositions: notes on the written word; Bookends: a year between the covers* (Wolsak and Wynn); and *Sex after 70 and other poems* (Bevalia Press). www.naomiwakan.com

freezing rain
through the taxi windows
Monets everywhere

Haiku Canada Review,
Oct. 2008

magnolias bloom
where we buried you
your scent

Betty Warrington-Kearsley writes short stories and poetry, some of which have been published in Canada and internationally. Her debut book of poems, *Red Lacquered Chopsticks,* was published in 2006. She lives in Ottawa.

the surface tension
supporting water striders
where the young boy drowned

Haiku Canada Newsletter,
XIX. 1, 2006

now alone at night
the deafening silence
of the stilled hamster wheel

New England Country Farmhouse,
chapbook, 2005

R. W. Watkins is probably best known for his ghazals, satirical verse, and essays on comics. His haiku have appeared in journals and anthologies since the mid 1990s, as well as in two dark-themed solo chapbooks. Outspoken on many issues, he resides in northeastern Newfoundland.

saying something inaudible
she lifts
a blazing marshmallow

Sayings for the Invisible,
Black Moss Press, 1988

the talk turns to mothers
tomato seeds
spill from her knife

The Ribs of Dragonfly,
Black Moss Press, 1984

From the late 1960s, Rod Willmot was a pioneer of haiku in English,
publishing widely and writing influential critical work. His Burnt Lake
Press published Nicholas Virgilio and John Wills. Born in Toronto, he
is now a translator (and speedskater) living in Montréal.

jazz club
scent of roses
from her neck

jazz club
her smoky lips kiss
the martini glass

Jeffrey Winke lives on the fifth floor of a 100+ year old brick former manufacturing building with an obstructed view of Lake Michigan where he writes haiku, haibun, and articles about heavy equipment moving dirt. In *The Doorman's Diary*, he records life as a jazz club doorman.

difficult to trace
patterns of swallows
in the evening sky

difficile à copier
les patrons des hirondelles
dans le ciel du soir

Klaus-Dieter Wirth, Germany, promotes haiku on an international level. Member of many international haiku societies, he has published in *Sommergras, Blithe Spirit, Gong, Chrysanthemum, Whirligig*. His last publication was the quadrilingual haiku book *Zugvögel/Migratory Birds/Oiseaux migrateurs/Aves migratorias*.

snowdrops peek through the earth
in the barn newborn lambs

alzheimer seminar
all depart
clutching every pamphlet

Haiku Canada Members' Anthology,
2005

Former Toronto librarian who found that the love of books carries over easily to haiku. Being a city person I continue to have difficulty creating haiku in the classic mode with references to nature.

Summer grasses—
cicadas' voices
fade into dusk

Forsythias—
too bright against
weeping willow

Sherry Zhou is a 13-year-old, very passionate young poet in grade 8.
She devours novels, loves art, and plays sports. She enjoys harmonizing
on the piano as well. She lives with her parents, a plethora of fish, and
three turtles in Palo Alto, California.

GEORGE SWEDE

So many memories. But, two do rise to the surface rather quickly and both involve the haiku weekends in the late 1970s and early 1980s held during Thanksgiving at Betty Drevniok's bunkhouse resort in Combermere, Ontario. The collegiality of the years immediately following the founding of Haiku Canada was similar to that found within hockey or baseball teams. We were united to win, not a championship, but the hearts and minds of readers by showing them what fine work was being done in the haiku form. At those fall weekends, discussions and planning would last hours past midnight. On one of those occasions, I promised to edit the *Canadian Haiku Anthology* (Three Trees Press, 1979). On another, Rod Willmot vowed to anthologize the best *Erotic Haiku* (Black Moss Press, 1983). Both anthologies made a huge splash (each launched at Toronto's foremost literary venue, Harbourfront), but, as with all splashes, they soon returned to the surrounding state of equilibrium.

Haiku Canada 2011, Newfoundland

weathered buddha
nestled : deep in
in periwinkle .

overabundance
of roses (beauty?)
not wasted